ALL MADRID

Editorial Escudo de Oro, S.A.

Puerta del Sol; in foreground, the Bear and the Madroño.

THE HISTORY AND GROWTH OF THE CITY OF MADRID

Origin of the name

It used be thought that the city had mythological origins, though these theories have since been proven to be the result more of a desire to emulate the history of other European cities than of true scientific rigour. Other beliefs alternatively had Madrid founded by Ocnus, Roman king and son of a goddess who named the city Mantua. Some said the city had originally been called Ursa («bear» in Latin), due to the large number of these animals to be found in the surrounding mountains and which, along with the madrona tree, has been the symbol of the city since medieval times. The truth is that its name dates

back to the Arab foundation of the city, and is derived from «Macher-it», that is, «mother of plentiful water», a reference to the abundance of water in the city and the land around it. After the city was taken by the Christians this word entered the Spanish language as «Magerit», over time changing to «Madrit», and finally becoming Madrid.

Medieval Madrid

Archaeological discoveries on the banks of the River Manzanares prove that people have been dwelling around what is now know as Madrid for more than one hundred thousand years. But the first recordings of Madrid's existence as a city are much more recent. Its foundation has been attributed to Muhammad I, son of

Remains of the ancient Arab city walls at Cuesta de la Vega; in the background, the apses of the cathedral.

Aerial view of the Plaza Mayor; in the background, the Royal Palace and the Teatro Real.

Plaza de la Villa.

the Emir of Cordoba Abderraman II, who in 852 or thereabouts erected a fortress on the site today occupied by the Royal Palace, to defend Toledo against Christian incursions from Leon and Castille. A Muslim population gathered around this fortress, living among the narrow winding streets of a small civil medina. Architectural evidence of this first period is found in the remains of the Arab city walls, preserved at Cuesta de la Vega behind the Cathedral. This evidence consists of traces of the city walls raised in the 9th and 10th centuries to strengthen the fortress and the medina, whose site extended slightly beyond the ground now occupied by the Royal Palace and Plaza de Oriente.

After Toledo was taken by Alphonse VI in 1085, Madrid came under Christian influence for good. Its new population settled in the original medina, sharing with existing Muslim residents, and were granted privileges to allow them to build Christian churches and monasteries. The fortress was converted into an occasional residence for the Kings of Castile who frequently came to hunt in the woods around the town. In 1202 the town was granted parliamentary privileges by Alphonse VIII. Fields of wheat, barley and vines were laid out alongside the ancient Arab waterwheels and gardens, increasing the commercial activity of the town, where by the 14th century several permanent markets were established. Of the many churches built during this period only two survive, San Nicolás de los Servitas and San Pedro el Viejo, now extensively altered, but both originally in the Mudejar style. The fortress itself was extended first by Henry II (1369-1379), who also built a hunting lodge in the neighbouring Pardo Mountains, and later by Henry IV (1454-1474). The latter conceded to the town the title of «*muy noble y muy leal*» (very noble and very loyal), and his sister, Isabel la Católica, his successor on the throne, was the first monarch to regulate life in the city.

4

Portrait of Philip II, by Alonso Sánchez Coello, and Portrait of Philip IV, by Velázquez (Prado Museum).

The Centuries of the House of Austria

With the crowing of Emperor Charles I of Spain and V of Germany (1516-1555), the House of Austria came into power in Spain. The emperor developed a great fondness for the town, and in 1534 he conceded it the crown from his shield. Madrid's greenery and wildlife created a privileged setting for hunting, his favourite pastime. And he too made extensive alterations to the fortress. But it was above all his son and successor, Philip II (1556-1598) who, by his decision in 1561 to move the court from Toledo to Madrid, made the city start to develop in earnest. From then on, except for a brief interruption between 1601 and 1606 when the court was moved to Valladolid, Madrid has always been the capital of Spain. This decision of Philip II was very controversial, since the Madrid of the time had only 20,000 inhabitants, very much less than Toledo, Seville or Valladolid. Not only did it not have a cathedral, it also lacked adequate infrastructures and other important services. However, its strategic position right in the centre of the Peninsula made it the ideal setting for the monarch to establish the heart of his country.

By the end of Philip II's reign, the population had already risen to 60,000. So in spite of the feverish building activity in the city at the time, this increase led to an enormous shortage of dwellings. The «Ley de Regalía y Aposento» (law of royal prerogative and lodging) was intended to resolve this problem by forcing city residents to give up part of their homes to accommodate distinguished guests arriving in the capital. However, all that happened was that to get round the law residents built houses that came to be known as «*casas a la malicia*» (houses of malice), deliberately built in such a way as to make division impossible.

The greatest work of architecture of Philip II's reign was located 49 km outside Madrid: the monastery of El Escorial, also housing the Royal Mausoleum. There are very few surviving palaces from this period, many having been

5

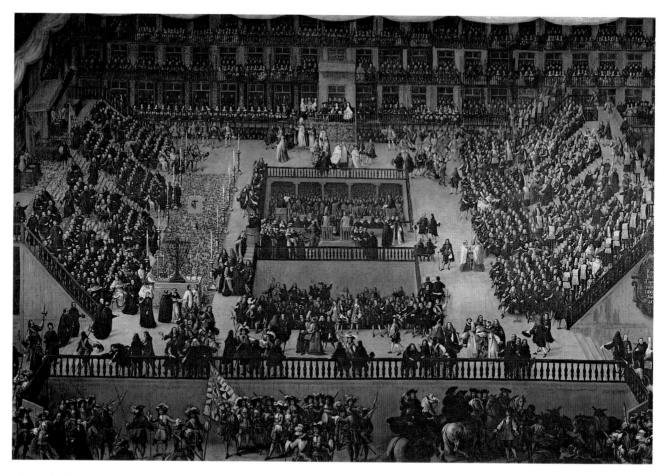

«Auto de Fe in the Plaza Mayor of Madrid», by Francisco Rizi (1650), (Prado Museum).

demolished or so altered that almost nothing of their original fabric remains. The few that do remain are mostly to be found in the Plaza de la Villa and its surrounding area: the Casa de los Lujanes, the Casa de Iván de Vargas and the Casa de Cisneros. Of note among religious buildings is the Monastery of the Descalzas Reales. During the reign of Philip III (1598-1621) extensive alterations were made to the city affecting both its planning and its architecture, with first Francisco de Mora and later his nephew, Juan Gómez de Mora, in charge of the works. These were the first municipal architects of the city, and they gave Madrid a definite style, more in keeping with its standing as a capital city: façades graced with uniform, small-framed windows, Flemish-style capitals and the use of red brick in combination with greyish stone on cornices and other decorative features. This reign was also responsible for the Plaza Mayor and improvements to the Calle Mayor.

Under Philip IV (1621-1665) Madrid grew to have 100,000 inhabitants. In 1625 Philip ordered the building of the wall that was to surround the capital until 1868. Its course ran along the present Calle de la Princesa to Plaza de Colón, and then continued along Paseo del Prado before ending at the Rondas of Toledo and Segovia. But Philip IV's most important building was the Palace of the Buen Retiro, built on the outskirts of the city in 1631. He put Velázquez in charge of its design and interior decoration, and Zurbarán was also commissioned to undertake parts of the work. Badly damaged during the War of Independence, the palace and its royal gardens were later to become the municipal park of El Retiro. Apart from this, old rural paths became new public ways - Calle Mayor and the streets of Atocha, Fuencarral, Hortaleza, Toledo and Segovia, and the new City Hall and Court Prison came into existence. Among the palaces from this era still standing are the Palace of the Duke of Uceda, the Palace of Cañete, the Casa de Lope de Vega and the Casa de las Siete Chimeneas. The 16th Century also saw the proliferation in Madrid

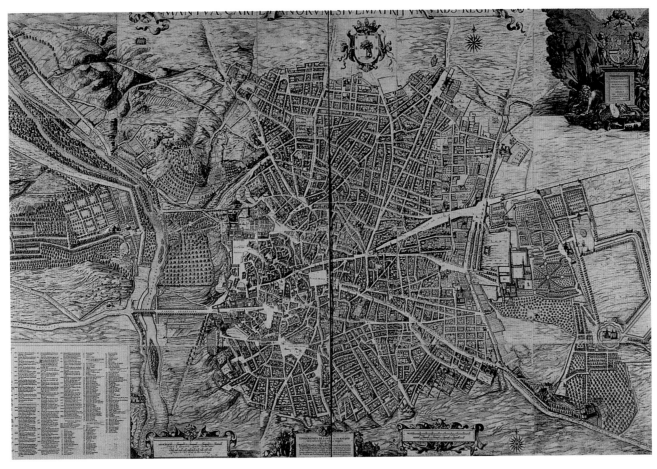

View over Madrid, painted in 1656, work of Pedro Texeira.

of churches and convents, as a result of the definitive establishment of the Court in the city. Another contributing factor here was the competitiveness of royalty, nobles, important gentlemen, religious orders and congregations in the sponsoring of new church buildings. The city's cramped layout did not easily lend itself to the construction of very showy buildings, its narrow streets making it almost impossible to appreciate pretentious façades such as those of the High Baroque style. This meant that architects made use of height to impress, having recourse to towers and domes rather than façades, and these were used as distinctive elements among the churches they designed. Many of these can still be seen: the Churches of San Isidro, las Carboneras del Corpus, la Carmen Calzado, las Trinitarias Descalzas, las Calatravas, San Ginés, las Agustinas Recoletas de Santa Isabel, las Bernardas de Sacramento, la Venerable Orden Tercera, San Antonio de los Alemanes, las Benedictinas de San Plácido, las Mercedarias Descalzas,

las Comendadoras de Santiago y San Sebastián, among others.

The Bourbons and the Enlightenment

With the Bourbons (the House of Bourbon came in with the victory of Philip of Anjou, crowned Philip V, after the War of the Spanish Succession, 1701-14) important reforms and building works took place that changed the face of the city. Enlightenment ideas made rulers more conscious of the need to modernise and Madrid, as capital of the Kingdom, became the main centre of attention. The 18th century therefore saw radical changes in the city's accessways, its surroundings, its infrastructures and its public services.

Under Philip V (1701-1746) institutions such as the Royal Academies, the Royal Library, the Hospice and the Cuartel del Conde Duque barracks came into being. The most striking innovation, however, was the new Royal Palace, built between 1737 and 1764 after the original fortress

«La pradera de San Isidro», painted around 1788 by Goya. In the background the outline of Madrid at the same time (Prado Museum).

was burnt down in 1734. The works on the palace in turn brought about the ordering of the streets in the vicinity along much wider and straighter lines.

To Ferdinand VI (1746-1759) we owe the present layout of the Paseo de las Delicias and the Ronda de Atocha, as well as the creation of the San Fernando Royal Academy of Fine Arts.

In the reign of Charles III (1759-1788), nicknamed the «rey mayor» (great king), further significant improvements were made. Aimed at making good the inadequacy of services and the shortage of resources, the Royal Factories of Glass, Tapestries and Porcelain made their first appearance. Other organisations whose origins date from this time were the Sociedades Económicas de Amigos del País (Economic Companies of Friends of the Country) (the best known being the Madrilenians), founded to encourage industry, agriculture and commercial development. In town planning matters, other measures were brought in, including the construction of the city's drainage system and its first street lighting, and the Paseo del Prado took on its present appearance. At one end, the Puerta de Alcalá was built (1778), and in 1785 a large neoclassical museum was built at its mid-point, to house a natural history collection: in 1819 this became the Prado Museum. Another highlight of Charles IV's reign (1788-1808) was the reconstruction of the Plaza Mayor, which had been almost totally destroyed by fire in 1790. By the end of

the 18th century, the population of Madrid was already nearing 170,000.

The aristocracy had taken to imitating the Court by building palaces with great emphasis on external details, using this as a sign of social status. Among such buildings from the first half of the 18th century surviving to the present day, although much changed in appearance, are the Palaces of Ugena, Miraflores and Perales, all works of the architect Pedro de Ribera. The most striking palaces, however, were built during the second half of the 18th century. Then, following neoclassical tenets, the nobility took great pleasure in their beautiful residences, which they enclosed behind railings and gardens. These not only enhanced the streets where they were built, but also improved the city environment in general. Examples of these are the Palaces of Liria, Buenavista and Vistahermosa. The best architects of the era were employed in their construction: Ventura Rodríguez, Francesco Sabatini, Juan de Villanueva and Antonio López Aguado among others.

Compared with the preceding century, there was a decrease in religious building, but more attention was given to the architectural quality of the few churches that were created during the century, making use of various artistic styles: in Baroque: San Cayetano, Montserrat, San José, San Miguel and Las Salesas Reales; in Transitional Neoclassical: San Marcos, Santiago and San

Francisco el Grande; and lastly, in pure Neoclassical: the Oratorio del Caballero de Gracia.

Madrid becomes middle class and demolishes its walls

The 19th Century began with the French invasion: on 2 May 1808 the city rose up against the French, but the revolt was brutally put down just one day later. There then followed the brief reign of Joseph I (1808-1814), brother of Napoleon Bonaparte. These were chaotic years for Spain, divided as it was between patriots and French sympathisers, while the text of the 1812 Constitution was being drafted in Cadiz. Madrid, however, was subject to a series of reforms principally aimed at decongesting its bustling historical centre. The end of the War of Independence heralded the reign of Ferdinand VII (1814-1833), under whom absolutism again held sway, and all the work of the Courts of Cadiz was undone. Immediately after this, during the long reign of Isabel II (1833-1870) the city underwent an almost total transformation.

As a result of the 1835 and 1855 laws of entailment on Church property, 38 of the 68 convents then in existence disappeared, and 540 properties belonging to religious orders were sold off. These properties fell into the hands of the up-and-coming middle classes. The opening up of streets and squares went on apace: of particularly importance were the reforms of the Puerta del Sol and the Plaza de Oriente. This period also saw the building of new houses and public buildings such as the Congreso de Diputados (parliament building), the Senate building, the National Library and the Bank of Spain. It also witnessed the construction of its main theatres: the sciences were encouraged by the creation of University Colleges and institutions such as the Madrid Athenaeum. The Cathedral of the Almudena and the Church of Santa Cruz were the only religious buildings of any significance erected in the 19th Century.

By the middle of this century, 280,000 people were crushed within the old city walls. To solve these demographic problems, a scheme known as the Castro Plan was approved. This involved the demolition of the walls and the planning of wide roads giving access to districts like Salamanca and Argüelles, where Madrid's new middle classes had settled. While new working class areas began to appear on the fringes of the city, in the centre the humbler classes were living crammed together in typical «corralas», many-storied dwellings built around a patio. These buildings became the protagonists of the «sainetes» or comedy sketches by Ramón de la Cruz, and the centre of «Madrid castizo» (the true Madrid).

«El 3 de mayo de 1808 en Madrid: los fusilamientos en la montaña del Principe Pío», by Goya (Prado Museum).

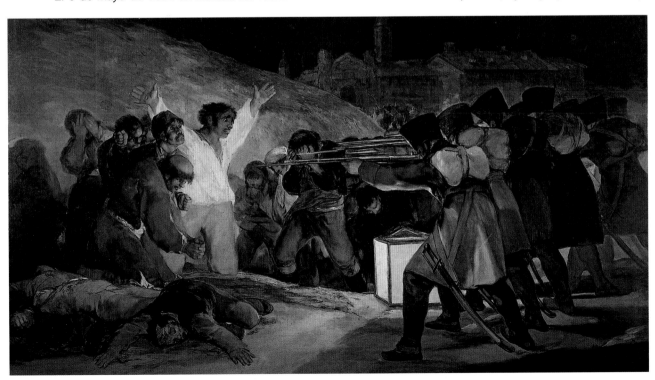

Aerial view of the Paseo de la Castellana and the Azca Complex.

Industrialisation advanced apace; small traditional factories existed side by side with modern services and industries: gas, the railway industries, electricity, metal foundries, the printing trade and the construction industry.

The 20th Century

By the start of the 20th century Madrid had a population of 580,000, and by 1930 this figure had increased still further to 950,000. In 1929, the City Council, concerned at the disproportionate growth taking place in the city, decided to bring some order to the matter: they put out a bid for a project to design the extension of the northern part of the city. As a result of this project, the Paseo de las Delicias de la Princesa changed its name

to the Paseo de la Castellana, extending to the Plaza de Castilla, and the Ciudad Lineal (the linear city) of Arturo Soria was also created. 1910 had already seen the inauguration of Gran Vía by Alphonse XIII, and in 1919 the first metro line running from Sol-Cuatro Caminos had come into service. Buildings such as the luxury Ritz and Palace hotels and the Palace of Communications had been built around the Plaza de la Cibeles. Works had begun on the Ciudad Universitaria (University City), conceived on the model of the American campus under the personal supervision of the king who had ceded the land. During the 2nd Republic (1931-1936), as had occurred a century earlier with the Parque del Retiro, the royal game reserve of the Casa de Campo passed into public ownership. The Civil War (1936-1939) was particularly bitter in Madrid. It opened the way to the government of General Franco, who was to direct the fate of Spain for the next 41 years from his residence in the Royal Palace of El Pardo, on the outskirts of the city. By 1950 Madrid had a million and a half inhabitants, and by 1960 this number had increased to more than two million. This outstanding growth was due partly to heavy immigration into the city but it was also the result of taking in surrounding villages, on the way to becoming the metropolitan area it is today. Also in the 50s new outlying districts were springing up, and sky-scrapers appeared in Plaza de España. After the Stabilisation Plan of 1959, Madrid entered a new stage of development, and frenetic activity began to make the city «fit» for the motorcar: Tree-lined boulevards disappeared, and in their place sprouted overpasses and underground parking lots; the M-30 was built right along the course of the old Abroñigal river. And later still the M-40, a new ring road, completely surrounded the city. In 1970 Madrid's population reached the three million mark, a figure that then remained steady or even fell slightly, although surrounding villages such as Majadahonda, Las Rozas, Boadilla del Monte, Alcorcón, Leganés and Getafe went on growing substantially. After the death of General Franco on 20 November 1975, Juan Carlos I was declared King of Spain and Head of State, and democracy was re-established. In the three last decades of the 20th century, and particularly since the early 1980s, the city was modernised. Existing areas such as La Castellana, the Plaza de Colón and the Plaza de Castilla were transformed, while new areas were forming with concentrations of the best examples of avant-garde architecture such as the Azca Complex and the Torres Puerta de Europa. But the foundations of a more habitable Madrid were also being laid: districts were being re-equipped, architectural heritage protected by special plans, public transport improved, a project for wholesale reorganisation brought in, old parks restored and new parks designed: and finally a new development plan was initiated that would ensure the present and future growth of the city on more human and rational lines. Apart from all this, recent developments have made Madrid one of the richest cities in the world in terms of art. These developments include the opening in 1986 of the Museo Nacional Centro de Arte Reina Sofía to exhibit *Guernica*, Picasso's most famous work, and more recently of the Museo Thyssen Bornemisza, the magnificent collections of the Prado Museum and other museums such as the San Fernando Royal Academy of Fine Arts.

Torre España.

Puerta del Sol.

PUERTA DEL SOL AND THE MONASTERIES OF THE DESCALZAS REALES

This square has always been one of the most popular areas of Madrid, and so has been the scene of important events in the history of the city and of Spain: the uprising of 2 May 1808, depicted in Goya's painting of the same name; the first gas lighting, switched on in 1830; the inauguration of the first line of the Metro, Sol-Cuatro Caminos, in 1919; and the proclamation of the Second Republic in 1931. It also contains **Kilometre 0** of the roads of Spain.

Originally, in the 15th century, this area was on the outskirts of the city, surrounded by a wall with a gate «facing the sun», hence its name. From 1560 onwards, various buildings, together with the bookshops, cheap eating houses and jewellers' shops established there, brought about a rivalry with the Plaza Mayor over which was the city centre. Later,

the popular **Mariblanca Fountain** was added, of which a copy remains on a column at one of the corners of the square.

It was during the reign of Isabel II when the definitive reforms of this area were carried out, giving it the elliptical shape it has today. The only original building to be preserved is the **Real Casa de Correos** (post office building), the work of Jaime Marquet in 1761, which between 1847 and 1979 served as the seat of the Ministerio de la Gobernación and later as the Office of the President of the Community of Madrid. Ever since the 19th century it has been the tradition on Old Year's Night to bring in the New Year to the sound of its clock striking.

In one corner, opposite the Calle del Carmen, a **statue in bronze of the bear and the madrona** represents the coat of arms of Madrid.

The streets of Carmen and Preciados, today pedestrianised and leading to the Plaza del Callao, are the

Puerta del Sol: the former Real Casa de Correos building, «kilometre zero», and the statue of the Mariblanca.

Monastery of the Descalzas Reales: façade and main stairway.

hub of busy commercial activity. Classical establishments rub shoulders with more modern shops, and it also houses the first branch to be opened by the popular department store, El Corte Inglés.

By taking these streets you can reach the **Monasterio de las Descalzas Reales** (Plaza de las Descalzas Reales 3), one of the most interesting places in the city due to its collection of magnificent artistic treasures. Founded by Princess Joan of Austria, daughter of Emperor Charles V, this monastery occupies a palace that formerly belonged to Alonso Gutiérrez, the imperial treasurer. When the Alcazar became the official residence of Philip II, the palace was placed at the disposal of his mother, the Empress Isabel, and it was here that the founder of the monastery was born in the summer of 1535, «in the cool rooms overlooking the large garden». The work of transforming the palace into a convent were directed by Antonio Sillero and Juan Bautista de Toledo (author of the original designs for El Escorial) from 1556 to 1564, and work was continued in the 17th century by Juan Gómez de Mora. The front of the church is an austere, beautiful composition in the style of El Escorial, over which is emblazoned the coat of arms of its founder.

For centuries, the wives and daughters of royalty and the aristocracy worshipped or were guests here, and this is the reason behind the extraordinary accumulation of works of art to be found in the convent, particularly from the 15th to the 17th centuries. Outstanding among these are the decoration of the staircase, with splendid effects of perspective, attributed to Claudio Coello and Ximénez Donoso, paintings by Peter Burgle I, Pandora de la Cruz, Zurbarán, Titian and Sanchez Coello, as well as a room adorned by tapestries based on cartoons by Rubens. In the monastery, in which nuns still live, you can also see the work of such religious painters as Pedro de Mena and Gregorio Hernández and a magnificent collection of liturgical ornaments.

15

Aerial view of the Plaza Mayor.　　　　　　*Casa de la Panadería and equestrian statue of Philip III.* ▷

PLAZA MAYOR

This was constructed by Juan Gómez de Mora, commissioned by Philip II, who wanted to build a great square which would give prestige to his kingdom. The site chosen was the former Plaza del Arrabal, the setting of an important market since the 16th century. Work began in 1617 and was completed two years later. The rational project, in Madrilenian Baroque style characteristic of the period of the Austrias, was an innovation in town planning in the city. The plans left standing the **Casa de la Panadería**, on whose ground floor was a bakery built by Diego Sillero in 1590. At present the former headquarters of this guild houses the Civil Registry. The remaining house immediately opposite is the former **Casa de la Carnicería**.

The square contains 136 houses, with 437 balconies from which 50,000 people were able to witness the many events held here, tourneys, bull fights, the proclamations of monarchs, royal weddings, autos-da-fe, executions and local festivities. The beatification and canonisation of San Isidro and other popular saints such as Santa Teresa de Jesus also took place here. The character of this square has remained unaltered over the years, and it still a meeting-place and the site of evening strolls of many Madrilenians, particularly lively on Sunday mornings due to the stamps and old coins market set up under its Colonnades. In its centre stands the **equestrian statue of Philip III**, sponsor of the building of the square, and the first monarch of the House of Austria to be born in Madrid. This work of Pietro Tacca, 1616, was initially placed in the Casa de Campo. It was moved to the square in 1847 after the wedding celebrations of Isabel II, during which the last bull run (corrida) was held in the square.

Nearby, between 1629 and 1643 in the Plaza de la

The colonnades of the Plaza Mayor provide the setting for many small shops.

Provincia, the **Palacio de Santa Cruz** was built; since 1850 it has been the headquarters of the Ministry of Foreign Affairs, formerly the Court Prison, following a design of Juan Gómez de Mora, also the architect of the Plaza Mayor. The main façade, an example of Madrilenian Baroque, is framed by two-spired towers, the brick used in them contrasting with the stone of the imposts, chains, balcony openings and central doorway, central decorative elements. Built to replace the old prison, in which Lope de Vega is said to have been held, due to its poor security, its opening ended the tradition of holding prisoners in the houses of ordinary citizens.

Collectors' stamp and coin market in the Plaza Mayor.

Arco de Cuchilleros, one of the access-ways to the Plaza Mayor. ▷

Madrid City Council.

PLAZA DE LA VILLA AND MEDIEVAL MADRID

An important square in the history of the city, for Madrid has been governed from here since time immemorial. The locals used to meet in the Church of San Salvador and were granted the right to organise their own local government in the 14th century by Alphonse XI. In this way, the Madrid City Council came into being and it was decided to build a **City Hall** on the site of the now demolished church. Executed in Madrilenian Baroque, the project was supervised by Juan Gómez de Mora, who made a start to its construction in 1640; it was then continued by José Villarreal, to be completed by Teodoro Ardemans in 1690. Since then, the building has remained unchanged except for a balcony over the Calle Mayor designed by Juan de Villanueva in 1787 added so that the Queen and her ladies could view the Corpus procession.

The square, irregular in shape and presided over by the **statue of Don Alvaro de Bazán**, Admiral of the «Invincible Armada», (Mariano Benlliure, 1888), also houses other unusual buildings. The oldest of these, dating from the end of the 15th century, is the **Torre y Casa de los Lujanes**. The tower is in the Mudejar style; the house preserves two ancient façades, the front façade overlooking the square and bearing the coat of arms of the Lujanes, and the lateral façade over the Calle del Codo, incorporating a pointed horseshoe arch.

Behind the City Council, and these days forming part of it, is the **Casa de Cisneros**, built in 1537 in the Plateresque style by Benito Jiménez de Cisneros, nephew of Cardinal Cisneros, whose main entrance is from Cordón Street. The interior of this palace, with its peaceful garden and home to a magnificent col-

Torre and Casa de los Lujanes.

lection of tapestries, was completely refurbished by Luis Bellido in 1910.

To the south of the Plaza de la Villa lies the old quarter of La Morería, whose labyrinth of tiny, irregular-shaped squares and winding streets allow the visitor a glimpse of the layout of the medieval city. To walk the little streets of this district, with their evocative names –Granado, Redondilla, Mancebos, Alfonse VI, or Alamillo, Morería or Paja squares– so full of history and legend, is to return to a Madrid recently reconquered, in which the Moorish population was confined within this area and from which period the district takes its name. It is certain that this district contained a mosque, probably situated on the site where, in 1312, Alphonse XI ordered the building of the Mudejar

Tower of the church of San Pedro el Viejo.

Church of San Andrés.

Church of San Pedro el Viejo, of which only the tower has survived. In the late-15th century, the district began to flourish once more and the palaces of the noble Lasso de Castilla, Vargas, Alvárez de Toledo and Lujanes families were constructed, only to be replaced during the 19th century by the dwellings which we can contemplate today.

Between the squares of La Paja and San Andrés is one of the most interesting architectural areas of the city, formed by the Church of San Andrés, the Chapel of the Bishop and the Chapel of San Isidro. The **Church of San Andrés** dates from the 12th century, but it was totally rebuilt in the 16th century and again after the Civil War. The **Capilla del Obispo** had its origin in the 16th century as the chapel of the Church of San Andrés. An essentially Gothic building, its magnificent great altarpiece, work of Francisco Giralte, and the tombs of the church's sponsor, Don Gutierre de Carvajal y Vargas and his parents, are in Renaissance

style. The adjoining **Chapel of San Isidro**, with its airy dome, was built in the mid-18th century to keep safe the relic of San Isidro, although his tomb was later moved to the basilica dedicated to the patron saint of Madrid in Toledo Street. Also in the Plaza de San Andrés is the **Museum of San Isidro**, established in the house where it is thought the saint died in 1172 and that belonged to Iván de Vargas, for whom San Isidro had worked as a labourer. On exhibition are archaeological remains found in the area, and there is a small chapel decorated with frescos by Zacarías González Velázquez.

Near the Church of San Pedro is the **Plaza Puerta Cerrada** whose name goes back to one of the gardens that were built into the old medieval city walls, once the market area. It has not lost its former liveliness, and today it is still one of the busiest squares in Madrid, with its many shops and restaurants.

At the other end of the district, in the Plaza de San

Francisco, rises the **Church of San Francisco el Grande**. Founded in the 13th century, when Saint Francis of Assisi personally chose this as the site for a modest monastery, it became a focal point towards which the city expanded, and when the monastery was demolished in the 18th century the church contained twenty-five chapels and the tombs of some forty illustrious figures. The new church was built in the Neo-Classical style popular at the time, according to the plans of Fray Francisco Cabezas, whose conception was of a circular building covered by an imposing dome 33 metres in diameter. However, it was completed in 1776 by Sabatini, who solved the problems caused by the enormous size of the dome. Its outstanding feature is the huge façade organised in two high storeys, supporting the dome. The interior contains «San Bernadino», one of Goya's earliest works.

Chapel of San Isidro.

Church of San Francisco el Grande.

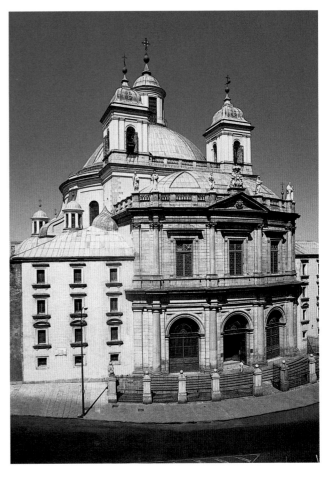

23

Plaza de Oriente and the Royal Palace.

THE PLAZA DE ORIENTE, THE ROYAL PALACE AND THE CATHEDRAL

Its name is due to the fact that the square adjoins the eastern front of the Royal Palace, and its construction to Joseph Bonaparte's wish to create a space from which the beauty of this monumental palace could be contemplated. Development of the square was completed in the time of Isabel II according to plans drawn up by Agustín Argüelles and Martin de los Heros. The central **statue of Philip IV** was laid in 1843 and is a beautiful 17th-century sculpture, in whose completion various artists worked: Pietro Tacca sculpted the bronze after the model by Martinez Montañés; the head is a copy of that of the equestrian portrait by Velazquez and Galileo Galilei calculated the centre of gravity to ensure the equilibrium of the statue. Subsequently,

the statues of other monarchs, originally intended for the balustrade of the Royal Palace, were placed in the gardens.

The buildings surrounding the square date back to the 19th century. One of the most interesting of these is the **Teatro Real**. In remote times, this was the site of the fountains and washing place of the district, also known as the Caños del Peral. In 1704, a group of travelling actors made their home here, giving origin to the theatre which stood here until the early-19th century. In 1818 this was pulled down due to its ruinous state and plans were drawn up by Antonio López Aguado for the Royal Theatre. Work on this was held up repeatedly until its eventual completion in 1850 by express order of Isabel II, and the theatre was inaugurated on 19 November of that year with a performance of Donizetti's «La Favorita». In the early the 20th century, however, it had to be

Plaza de Oriente: equestrian statue of Philip IV, façade and interior of the Teatro Real.
(Image of the interior: Javier del Real, Teatro Real).

Real Monasterio de la Encarnación.

closed since a subterranean spring was causing serious damage and it was in danger of collapse. In 1965 it opened again as a concert hall and music conservatory, and finally, in 1997, after ten intense years of restoration work, it was again inaugurated, this time as an opera house. It contains some lovely public rooms and its stage, with facilities boasting the very latest in technology, is one of the largest and best equipped in the world.

On the other side of the square, behind the Gardens of Cabo Noval, is the **Real Monasterio de la Encarnación**. Founded by Queen Margaret of Austria, spouse of Philip III, it took five years to complete the construction of the convent, under the direction of Juan Gómez de Mora, which was blessed in 1616 in solemn ceremony. The front, harmoniously constructed in beautiful ashlar and brick, became the model for the churches of the Carmelites for several decades, with slight variations. The church suffered a fire in the mid-18th century and Ventura

Reliquary containing the blood of San Pantaleón.

Sabatini Gardens.

Palacio del Senado.

Royal Palace.

Rodríguez, commissioned to restore the interior, employed a wealth of jasper, marble and bronze in accordance with the tastes of Bourbon times. The church is popular in Madrid as it contains a reliquary containing the blood of Saint Pantaleón, which liquefies every 27 July. Besides this, the museum contains many more reliquaries and an excellent collection of paintings, sculptures and religious art, as well as a remarkable collection of liturgical objects and other interesting items accumulated through the gifts of the noblewomen who worshipped at the convent or through the donations of its illustrious guests.

During the 2nd Republic, the land to the north of the Royal Palace, formerly occupied by the palace stables, was transformed into the **Sabatini Gardens**. This peaceful park, with its hedges laid out in geometric figures, bears the name of Francesco Sabatini, one of the favourite architects of Charles III: he was granted the title of the King's Master Architect, among others. And it was for the king that he carried out his most important commissions, including the extension to and refurbishment of the Royal Palace and that of the Palace of El Pardo and the Puerta de Alcalá. The building in front of the gardens at the other side of Bailén is the **Palacio del Senado**, whose main entrance is in the Plaza de la Marina Española. It occupies the site of a former convent that was totally rebuilt in the early 19th century, in 1814, after the War of Independence, becoming the meeting place of the kingdom's Cortes Generales.

The entrance to the **Royal Palace** is in Calle Bailén, through the spacious Patio de Armas. The old Alcazar, "fortress", a cold and inhospitable 9th-century Moorish construction, extended by the kings of the House of Austria, was completely burnt down on Christmas Eve 1734 in one of the fastest and most terrible fires recorded. The flames devoured a

Throne Room. (Copyright © Patrimonio Real).

Royal Pharmacy. (Copyright © Patrimonio Real).

Royal Armoury. (Copyright © Patrimonio Real).

marvellous collection of paintings and objets d'art, but also gave the new Bourbon dynasty the opportunity to fashion a building more appropriate as the setting for the official activities of the country and as the royal residence, following the example set by the principal courts of Europe. Philip V summoned Filippo Juvara from Italy and proposed that he build a huge building comparable to the Palace of Versailles in the style of Bernini's project for the Louvre, though, due to its size, located outside the city centre. Shortly after completing the plans, Juvara died and the king commissioned his pupil Giovanni Battista Sachetti to carry out the work, imposing the condition that he must use the site of the old Alcazar.

Sachetti began construction with the intention that what the palace lost in extension should be gained in height, and ensured that the new building should

Sala de Porcelana. (Copyright © Patrimonio Real).

be fire-proof by using only stone as his materials. The first stone was laid in 1738. Building, in which the architects Sabatini and Ventura Rodríguez also intervened, was completed in 1764, and the first monarch to make his residence here was Charles III. The overall design is in the style of Baroque Classicism, whilst there is a mixture of French and Italian influences in the elements used its in construction and decoration. This splendid building forms a quadrilateral made up of four almost identical façades and the series of pillars and embedded columns and the combination of granite and white stone are perhaps the most outstanding features of its composition. The solid basement of bossed ashlar which makes up the ground floor gives emphasis to the classical elegance of the main floor, which features embedded supports and finely-designed windows between the columns. The whole is crowned by a balustrade.

The Palace is now used for state occasions, whilst part houses a museum which cannot be missed by visitors, for it offers the chance to appreciate one of the best-furnished palaces of Europe. In fact, the original furniture has been conserved, and outstanding amongst its dependencies being the rooms decorated by Gasparini, formerly the private chambers of Charles III, the throne room and the state dining room. Innumerable works of art adorn the Palace: there are ceilings decorated by Corrado Giaquinto, Tiepolo and Mengs, and works by Goya, Watteau, Van der Weyden, Bosch, Velazquez and Caravaggio. The demands of protocol and the social life of the monarchs caused a wealth of sumptuous objects to be accumulated here, now part of the Palace collections, and which were enriched over various reigns. These collections have incalculable artistic, historic and documentary value, containing some of the most important pieces of their type;

Gardens of the Royal Palace, El Campo del Moro.

tapestries, porcelain, gold and silver work, royal mantles, religious robes, clocks, sculptures, bronzes, chandeliers, furniture, carpets, etc.

Several monographic museums, each with extraordinary collections, are housed within the building: the **Music Museum**, with a Stradivarius quintet; the **Royal Library**, with more than 300,000 volumes and incunabulae; the **Royal Pharmacy**, with a 17th-century alchemy laboratory; the **Royal Armoury**, a collection founded by Philip II to gather together and conserve his and his father's weapons, considered one of the finest in the world of its type; and the **Carriage Museum**, a collection of vehicles used by the monarchs from the 16th to the 20th centuries, servants' uniforms, saddles and horse-riding equipment.

This museum is set in the gardens of the Royal Palace, known as **El Campo del Moro**. Restored in the late 19th century, they are in the English style with elegant fountains, paths bordered by hedges and exuberant vegetation that form a contrast with the extensive areas laid out in lawn.

The site on which the Palacio Peal stands is one of the most beautiful areas of the city and among the most splendid both architecturally and in terms of town planning as, when construction began, the plans also included consideration of the surrounding area. The Cathedral of the Almudena and Bailén, and also the viaduct that crosses the low-lying area at Segovia, were all designed at the same time as the palace, although not executed until much later.

Cathedral of the Almudena.

Viaduct.

Work started on the **Cathedral of the Almudena** in the last quarter of the 19th century and at that time only its Neo-Romanesque crypt was built. The design, by the Marquis of Cubas, is in an eclectic style with mediaeval sources of inspiration. Its verticality and medieval quality is in stark contrast with the horizontal lines and classical style of the adjacent Royal Palace. The main façade, with two identical, symmetrical towers, was finally completed in 1960, with huge differences from the original plans. The Cathedral, however, was not finished until 1993, and was consecrated that same year by Pope John Paul II; until then, the Basilica of San Isidro had been used as a Cathedral. The church is dedicated to the Virgin of La Almudena, patron saint of the city, and worshipped there since earliest times. Legend has it that during the Moorish occupation the Christian inhabitants hid the statue of the Virgin in a fold of the wall («almudaina» in Arabic) or in a grain store («almudit») nearby, and it was miraculously discovered when Alphonse VI reconquered Madrid on 9 November 1085. Since then, the statue of the Virgin Mary has received the name of Almudena. a popular girl's name in Madrid.

The construction of the **Viaduct** over Segovia Street, joining the area of the Palace with Vistillas, was not completed either until the end of the 19th century, when it was executed in iron. The present viaduct, inaugurated in 1942, is made of reinforced concrete. Looking out from the viaduct you can enjoy a lovely view that stretches into the distance as far as the Guadarrama Mountains.

The Corrala in Mesón de Paredes, Street.

THE BASILICA OF SAN ISIDRO, THE PUERTA DE TOLEDO AND THE AREA ROUND THE RASTRO

Between the streets of Toledo in the west and Atocha in the east, and the Rondas of Toledo, Valencia and Atocha in the south, following the line of the 17th century city walls, lie the districts of La Latina, Lavapiés and Embajadores: together these make up one of the most typical areas of Madrid, known also as the «Madrid *castizo*» (purest Madrid). The «castizo» culture arose in the 18th century, when the city was undergoing tremendous growth and the rising classes were building their palaces and adopting sophisticated French styles; in contrast, the humbler classes were becoming more self-confident, bold and presumptuous in the face of their rich new neighbours, even inventing a way of talking characterised by its playing on words and ironic retorts. These were the first «castizos» of Madrid. Today, however, the words have taken on a wider meaning, «castizos» now being considered to mean «Madrid stock, through and through». These areas do not have the monumental character of other parts of Madrid, since they were inhabited basically by craftsmen and modest employees, and their main interest comes from their folkloric appearance. Their «corralas», dwellings in flats laid out around a large interior patio and linked on each floor by a gallery, were the typical houses of this area. Here residents led a very com-

Plaza de Lavapiés.

munal kind of life, and their patios were often used to mount verbenas (festivals) and put on theatre performances, particularly «sainetes» or comedy sketches and «zarzuelas» or light operas. The **Corrala de la Calle Mesón de Paredes**, between Sombrerete and del Tribulete Street, and restored as a National Monument, is amongst the most famous examples: its stage inspired the zarzuela «La Revoltosa» by Ruperto Chapí.

The Plaza de Lavapiés and the Plaza de Cascorro are the main focal points of this area. The **Plaza de Lavapiés**, whose name refers to a fountain that had once existed there, was the centre of Jewry in former times. It was the most typical place in this district full of «Manolos» and «Manolas», diminutives

from Manuel and Manuela, the name most commonly used for baptising the children of converted jews which also came to be applied to young boys and girls from the lower sections of the city population. The **Plaza del Cascorro** owes its name to a battle fought in Cuba in 1896, and is presided over by the statue of Eloy Gonzalo, a hero of this battle who was born in Lavapiés. The statue was executed by Aniceto Marinas y López Salaberry in 1901, and shows the soldier just before he set fire with petrol to the fort where a group of insurgents was hiding. The rope looped round his waist was so his companions could pull him out if he died in the act.

Between the Plaza del Cascorro and the Ronda de Toledo in the area around Ribera de Curtidores, the

Plaza del Cascorro: monument to Eloy Gonzalo.

Plaza del Cascorro: monument to Eloy Gonzalo.

Rastro, the most famous open market in Madrid is held, on Sundays and holidays. Its origins go back to the 16th century, when the area contained the slaughterhouse, known as the «rastro», around which other traders established their businesses. These were followed in the 19th century by the second-hand clothes and junk dealers, who in turn gave way to antique shops and auction houses. However, the Rastro of the present day is chiefly characterised by the infinity of street dealers selling absolutely everything and the crowds of people who, looking out for a bargain, or simply enjoying the colourful scene, fill these streets with bustling life.

The most important monuments in this area are the Basilica of San Isidro and the Puerta de Toledo.

The **Basilica of San Isidro**, very much loved by Madrilenians because it served for centuries as their cathedral, is located in Toledo Street. Two Jesuit architects, Francisco Bautista and Pedro Sánchez, were the designers of this church, formerly the chapel of the Colegio Imperial de la Compañía de Jesús. Its grand façade, covered by enormous columns, can scarcely be seen from the front due to the narrowness of the street, but viewed from the side it gains in perspective and effect. At its centre, in a niche, are images of the patron of the City, San

The Rastro.

Basilica of San Isidro.

Isidro, and his wife, Santa María de la Cabeza. Its wrought iron gate is crowned by a two-headed eagle, symbol of the dynasty of the House of Austria, founders of the College. Inside, kept in twin urns on the great altar, are the mortal remains of San Isidro and his wife. Although the building of the church was initiated in 1622, its interior decoration had to wait for its completion by Ventura Rodríguez until the mid-18th century.

The **Puerta de Toledo** was started during the brief reign of Joseph Bonaparte, and the work completed a few years later, but in the reign of Ferdinand VII to whom it is dedicated. It is in Neo-Classical style, and crowned by Allegories of Spain protecting the Arts.

Puerta de Toledo.

Gran Vía with Calle de Alcalá. Church of San José.

Aerial view of the Calle de Alcalá. ▷

ALCALÁ - THE STREET AND THE GATE

Alcalá is without a doubt the most famous street in Madrid, and also one of the longest, although the section with greatest interest for us lies between the Puerta del Sol and the Plaza de la Independencia. It came into existence in the 17th century, the result of the gradual inclusion within the city limits of the different sections of the path taken by University students coming and going from Alcalá de Henares. The first of the original features of the road to disappear were its gardens, olive groves, taverns and carriage hiring establishments, to be replaced in the era of the Casa de Austria by hospitals, convents and churches. It was later extended, and many of its original buildings were replaced. From these early days only the **Church of the Calatravas** remains, a monastery founded to

accommodate women whose relatives, members of the military order of Calatrava, were fighting in the Crusades. The monastery buildings were demolished in 1872, except for the church whose façade was restored by Juan de Madrazo in 1886. Inside is an original altar with a Baroque altarpiece, work of Churriguera.

A little further on, alongside the Gran Vía, the **Church of San José** also lost its original convent. Built in 1733 by Pedro de Ribera on the site of an earlier church, its façade contains features typical of this artist, with brickwork framed by chains of stone and, above all, the notable vertical axis which, beginning at the porch, rises up to the very top of the building. In the second half of the 18th century this formerly religious street took on a financial character: a precursor of this change being the building of the **Real**

Real Casa de la Aduana.

Casa de la Aduana (customs house), very near to the Puerta del Sol, which today houses the Ministry of the Economy. Planned in 1769 by Sabatini and commissioned by Charles III, it has a sober and sparsely decorated façade. Charles III also gave a very substantial impetus to the arts when he acquired the palace of the banker Juan de Goyeneche at number 11, built by Churriguera in 1710, to accommodate the **San Fernando Royal Academy of Fine Arts** created in 1752 by his brother and successor, Ferdinand VI. To reflect this change of function, the original Baroque gateway was modified by Diego de Villanueva in accordance with the Neo-Classical taste of the times. Today, the museum of the Academy, of which Goya was joint director and through whose doors passed Picasso and Dalí amongst many other illustrious contemporaries, is one of the richest of its kind in the country in painting and sculpture, both Spanish and foreign. Its collections also include drawings, engravings, furniture, silver items, porcelain and other sumptuary arts from several different eras.

The last great overhaul of the Calle Mayor happened at the start of the 20th century, when banks and large companies favoured it as the site for their headquarters, putting up buildings that converted it into one of the most elegant streets in the city. But there was also room for art, culture and entertainment, as shown by the building of the **Círculo de Bellas Artes** at number 42, work of Antonio Palacios in 1926, with a magnificent cafe topped off with painted ceilings, chan-

San Fernando Royal
Academy of Fine Arts:
room, «La Tirana» by
Goya, and «Fray
Jerónimo Pérez» by
Zurbarán
*(Archivo Fotográfico Real
Academia de Bellas Artes
de San Fernando).*

Calle de Alcalá.

deliers and large columns. Also here is the **Madrid Casino** at number 15, the work of López Salaberry in 1910, with modernist elements both on its façade and decorating its beautiful interior stairway.

At the end of this stretch is the **Puerta de Alcalá**, the gateway that is one of the most famous monuments in Madrid and one of those that best represents it. Commissioned in 1778 as a triumphal arch by King Charles III in his desire to endow the city with worthy entrances, the work was entrusted to Francisco Sabatini. The design is in the purest Neo-Classical style, broken only by the sculptural decorations by Francisco Gutiérrez and Roberto Michel. Built in granite and white stone from Colmenar. It consists of five arches, the two outside topped with lintels and the other three semi-circular, whose central column appears to be higher due to the attic rising above it.

Madrid Casino.

Puerta de Alcalá. ▷

43

Plaza de Murillo.

Fountain of Apollo.

PASEO DEL PRADO

Always a popular area for walks, this zone was formerly part of the outskirts of the city, a pleasant spot with trees and gardens watered by the stream which ran from north to south. So it was throughout the 17th century, but in the 18th it was converted into an exponent of the illuminated ideas of the time by Charles III and his minister, the Count of Aranda. This involved the creation of a scientific and cultural area harmonising aspects of utility, beauty and diversion. Plans for this transformation were drawn up by Jose Hermosilla, who levelled land, channelled and covered the stream and altered the layout of the plantations to maintain the shadows of their trees whilst leaving a wide avenue, for which Ventura Rodríguez designed the great monumental fountains we can now admire: the **Cuarto Fuentes** fountain in the Plaza de Murillo; the **Fountain of Neptune** with its representation of the sea god on a carriage shaped like a conch drawn by sea horses; the **Fountain of Apollo** with the god of music and poetry on a high pedestal surrounded by the Four Seasons; and lastly, the **Fountain of Cibeles** showing the Greek god of fertility in a carriage drawn by lions. The last of these is located in one of the most beautiful spots in Madrid, not only for to its views over the avenues and passages that meet in the square, but also because of the noble buildings all around it; this fountain is also the meeting place of the followers of Real Madrid, the city's main football team, whenever it wins a match. Followers of Atlético de Madrid, the other important city club, on the other hand, use the Fountain of Neptune for the same purpose.

Though never finally built, a columned arcade was planned on one side of the avenue, in which there were to be cafes and chocolate shops. The other side was devoted to research buildings, with the construction of the Botanical Gardens and the Natural

Fountain of Neptune.

History Museum, now the Prado Museum, both designed by Juan de Villanueva in the Neo-Classical style which dominates the entire width of the avenue and the gardens, fountains and Prado. Even today, the avenue retains its original character as a promenade, and is always full of visitors to the museums. This is a most pleasant spot due to the width of the avenue and the gardens, fountains and magnificent buildings lining it. In the Plaza de la Cibeles, next to Calle Alcalá are the **Bank of Spain** and the **Palace of Buenavista**. The latter, created in 1874 by José Echegaray, dramatist and politician and subsequently Minister of Taxation, was erected between 1884 and 1891 by Eduardo Adaro and Severiano Sainz de Lastra in a style inspired by Italian and French palace architecture. The Palace of Buenavista is today the seat of the Headquarters of the Army, and was erected at the end of the 18th century by Juan Pedro Arnal as a residence for Cayetana de Alba, the Duchess immortalised by Goya, who died without ever

seeing it completed. It later passed into the ownership of Manuel Godoy, Charles IV's Prime Minister.

On the other side of the square is the **Palace of Linares**, one of the most striking examples of 19th century palace architecture. This is the work of Charles Colubi, who built it between 1873 and 1883 at the orders of José de Murga, a businessman raised to nobility with the title of Marquis of Linares. At present, part of the palace is occupied by the Casa de América, a Latin American cultural centre.

But undoubtedly the most historical building in the Plaza de la Cibeles is the **Palace of Communications**, built in 1904 by Antonio Palace to accommodate the Post Office Headquarters. Precisely due to its monumental scale, the profuse sculptural decoration of its façade and the cathedral-like formality of its towers, the building soon came to be known among Madrilenians by the nickname «Nuestra Señora de las Comunicaciones» (Our Lady of the Communications). Inside,

Fountain of Cibeles.

Fountain of Cibeles and Bank of Spain. ▷

Façade and interior of the Palacio de Linares.

you can admire its beautiful glass dome or visit the **Postal and Telegraphic Museum** (entrance in Montalbán). After completing this work, the Galician architect Antonio Palacios was offered many other commissions, and he imposed his personal style on the Madrid being built during the start of the 20th century: some of the most important of these are: in Alcalá, the Círculo de Bellas Artes, the Banco Central and the Casa Palazuelo, the latter just behind the Palace of Communications; and in Gran Vía, the Casa Matesanz and the Alfonso XIII Hotel.

Further along from the Palace of Communications, at Paseo del Prado 5, is a building dating from 1915 and planned by José Espelius, the **Naval Museum** where you can trace the history of Spanish navigation and admire a splendid collection of cartography. Two other museums in this area must be mentioned, apart from the Prado, the Thyssen-Bornemisza and the Centro de Arte Reina Sofía. The first is the **National Museum of Decorative Arts** (Montalbán 12), with very extensive collections from across the centuries, recreating domestic environments from different regions of Spain from the Renaissance to the 19th century. The second is the **Army Museum** (Méndez Núñez 1), occupying one of the only two buildings to have survived to present times from the palace of the Buen Retiro built by Philip IV, as well as also preserving the Salón de Reinos (Room of kingdoms), whose ceiling is decorated with the shields of all the kingdoms that then came under the Crown of Spain.

In Plaza de la Lealtad, the memory of the slaughter of the hundreds of Madrilenians who in May 1808 rebelled against the Napoleonic troops is honoured in the **Monument to the Unknown Soldier**, a granite monolith with an urn that holds the mortal remains of many of these victims. At one side of this square rises **The Stock Exchange** built in 1884 to a plan by the architect Repullés y Vargas, taking his inspiration from the Vienna Stockmarket. On the other side of the square is the **Hotel Ritz**, work of the French architect Charles Mewes, which opened in 1910. Shortly afterwards, in 1912, next to the adjoining Plaza de Cánovas del Castillo, the **Hotel Palace**, another elegant and luxurious hotel planned by the Belgian architectural firm León Monnoyer et fils, was inaugurated.

Opposite the Hotel Palace, at Paseo del Prado 8, the nineteenth-century Villahermosa Palace was totally remodelled by Rafael Moneo to accommodate the **Museo Thyssen-Bornemisza**, which opened its doors

Palace of Communications.

Exhibition room in the Naval Museum. (Archivo Fotográfico Museo Naval).

The Stockmarket Building.

to the public in 1992. This houses one of the best private collections of painting in the world, brought together by Heinrich Thyssen, a German magnate born in 1875, and his son, the Baron Von Thyssen, throughout the entire 20th century. Its collection, containing works from the 14th century up to the present day, complements those of its neighbours, the Prado Museum and the Centro de Arte Reina Sofía since, in a way, it fills in the gaps of the other two collections. Outstanding among the numerous master works it houses are the *Diptych of the Annunciation* by Jan Van Eyck, *Portrait of Giovanna Tornabuoni* by Ghirlandaio, *Young Horseman in a Landscape* by Carpaccio and *Saint Catherine of Alexandria* by Caravaggio. The 17th and 18th centuries

Museo Thyssen-Bornemisza.

are represented by artists such as Rubens, Van Dyck, Pieter de Hooch, Watteau, Boucher and Chardin. From the 19th century there are pictures by Realists like Courbet, Impressionists like Degas, Manet, Monet, Renoir, Pisarro and Sisley, Post Impressionists like Tolouse-Lautrec, Cézanne, Van Gogh and Gauguin, an important collection of North American artists and three Goyas. From the 20th century there are works representing all artistic movements, with figures such as Picasso, Miró, Matisse, Klimt, Schiele, Nolde, Mondrian, Magritte, Kandinsky, Paul Klee, Max Ernst, Dalí, Rothko, Pollock, Edward Hopper and Francis Bacon.

On the other side of the Paseo del Prado stands a

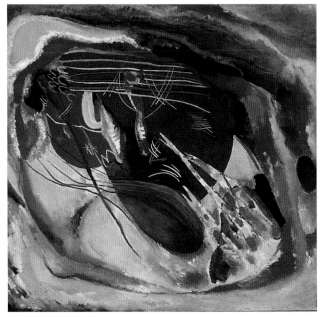

«Painting with three spots», Wassily Kandinsky (1914).
(© Museo Thyssen-Bornemisza, Madrid).

Prado Museum.

«El Caballero de la mano en el pecho» by El Greco. ▷

great Neo-Classical building, the work in 1785 of Juan de Villanueva. It was first destined to be a Museum of Natural Sciences, but finally inaugurated in 1819 as the Royal Museum, apparently due to a decision of Ferdinand VII influenced, it would seem, by his second wife María Isabel de Braganza. And so what we know today as the **Prado Museum** came into being. Its first collection consisted of 311 pictures from the valuable royal art collection initiated by the Emperor Charles V. Its collections were gradually built up through royal contributions, pictures from «entailed» convents and private donations. In 1868, when Isabel II was dethroned, the Royal Museum changed its name and became today's Prado Museum. Along with this change of name, its contents went on to become property of the State.

Already extended some years ago to take in the nearby Casón del Buen Retiro (Alfonso XII, 28), in 1999 the museum initiated a new extension and reforms of its facilities. This will allow more room for its collections, so extraordinary both in number and in quality, thus making it one of the best arts centres in the world.

Its painting collection, ranging from Romanesque to Goya, includes the most complete collection of Spanish painting, particularly from the 17th and 18th centuries, and a valuable representation of non-Spanish painting including master works by Fra Angelico (the work *Annunciation*), Andrea Mantegna (*The Death of the Virgin*), Raphael (*The Holy Family of the Lamb* and *The Cardinal*), Titian (*The Emperor Charles V at the battle of Mühlberg*), Tintoretto (*Lavatorio*), Veronese (*Moses*

saved from the water), Caravaggio (*David victorious over Goliath*), Brueghel (*The Triumph of Death*), Rubens, of which the museum has more than 80 works, among them *The Three Graces*, Rembrandt (*Artemisa*), Van der Weyden (*The Fall* and *The Descent from the Cross*), Bosch (*The Garden of Earthly Delights*) and Dürer (*Self Portrait* and the two pictures *Adam* and *Eve*).

The museum's Spanish painting includes half of the entire work of Velázquez, outstanding among whose canvases are *Las Meninas*, *La rendición de Breda*, *Villa de Médicis*, *Las hilanderas* and *Los borrachos*. There is also a very complete representation of the work of Goya on exhibition, with master works like the two «Majas», *La familia de Carlos IV*, *El 3 de mayo de 1808 en Madrid: los fusilamientos en la montaña del Príncipe Pío*, *El 2 de mayo de 1808 en Madrid: la lucha con los mamelucos* and his «Black Series». Mention must also be made of painters like El Greco (*El Caballero de la mano en el pecho*, *El bautismo de Cristo* and *La Resurrección*, among other works), Murillo (*La Sagrada Familia del pajarito*, *Los niños de la concha*, *El sueño del patricio Juan*), Ribera (*El sueño de Jacob*, *Magdalena penitente*), Zurbarán (*Visión de San Pedro Nolasco*, *Santa Casilda*), Pedro de Berruguete (*Auto de Fe*), Alonso Cano, Luis de Morales, Juan de Juanes, Alonso Sánchez Coello and Juan Carreño, among many more.

«Las lanzas» (the lances), popular name of the painting entitled «La rendición de Breda» by Velázquez.

«Las Meninas» by Velázquez, is one of the most harmonious and exquisitely balanced works of art ever painted.

«La maja desnuda» is one of the most popular works by Goya.

«La Concepción de El Escorial» moving image of the Virgin, by Murillo.

An extensive collection of sculpture, amounting to more than 500 pieces, and other priceless objects such as the Treasure of the Delfín, complete the heritage of the museum. The so-called Treasure of the Delfín is a magnificent collection of dinner services and porcelain that belonged to the eldest son of Louis XIV, heir to the French crown but who died before coming to the throne.

Between the Prado Museum and the Casón del Buen Retiro is the **Church of San Jerónimo el Real**, of very ancient origins. In 1462, Henry IV of Castile founded a Hieronymite monastery on the old route to El Pardo. In 1501 the Catholic Monarchs, due to the deterioration which this monastery had suffered, decided to rebuild it on the site it presently occupies. Work was completed on this Gothic construction in 1505, and in 1510 the first court of Ferdinand the Catholic was assembled here. Since that time, the church has been the traditional scene of the investiture of the princes of Asturias, the proclamation of kings and queens, royal weddings and other solemn occasions.

«Saint George slaying the Dragon» by Rubens.

Church of San Jerónimo el Real.

The Villanueva Pavilion, in the Botanical Gardens.

Ministry of Agriculture.

It was also a place of retreat for royalty, for since the time of Charles I there has been an «Old Room» here, where monarchs resided in times of mourning and during Lent. Over the centuries, the building was extended until it became the original nucleus of the great Palace of El Buen Retiro. The 19th century was a period of great suffering for the Church and Sant Jeronimo's was partially destroyed. Later, at the desire of Isabel II, it was restored by Narciso Pascual y Colomer in a style which took its inspiration from Late-Gothic Castilian architecture.

To the south of the Prado Museum extends the **Royal Botanical Garden**, created by Juan de Villanueva according to the Neo-Classical taste of the era and opened in 1781 by Charles III, whose statue presides over this pleas in which the plantings are organised into geometric figures, circles and squares, on the topmost of which was built the Villanueva Pavilion, used as greenhouse and library. This upper terrace was reorganised in the mid-19th century, its rationalism giving way to a romantic garden with the creation of a more natural landscape. The other two terraces are preserved with the same character as that in which they were created: the first, known as «the squares», devoted to the cultivation of medicinal plants, and the second, known as «the schools», where the plants are arranged from the most primitive up to the most highly developed.

The southern end of the Paseo del Prado comes out into the Plaza del Emperador Carlos V, which houses three historical buildings: the Ministry of Agriculture, Puerta de Atocha Railway Station and the Museo Nacional Centro de Arte Reina Sofía.

The headquarters of the **Ministry of Agriculture** was built in 1893 by Ricardo Velázquez, with the cooper-

Tropical garden inside Puerta de Atocha Station.

ation of the painter Zuloaga. The building's main features are its portico of columns sustained by caryatids, the glazed slabs of its upper floor, and the two enormous sculptures that crown the work, representing trade and industry (initially the building served as headquarters of the Ministry of Trade).

Puerta de Atocha Railway Station, located on the site of one of the old city gates of Madrid, was inaugurated in 1851. It was the first railway station in Madrid, and the popular «tren de la fresa», (strawberry train) that operated the Madrid-Aranjuez line, started from here. Destroyed by fire, it was reconstructed in 1892 in iron and glass to a design by Albert de Palacio, who gave it two platform buildings. Just one century later, in 1992, it was refurbished to allow it to host the high speed line (AVE).

The **Museo Nacional Centro de Arte Reina Sofía** (MNCARS) is installed in the former General Hospital of San Carlos, a project conceived by Charles III and carried out to a design by Sabatini. More recently, the main façade has had glass towers added, from which there are astonishing views over the area. Dedicated to contemporary art in all its forms, with both Spanish and foreign works represented, its funds come basically from the collections of the former MEAC and from the acquisitions of the MNCARS itself, but also from important legacies such as those of Salvador Dalí and Joan Miró. From Dalí, the following works must be highlighted *Muchacha en la ventana, Arlequín* and *El gran masturbador*; various paintings and sculptures of Joan Miró's last period are on show, dating from 1967 to 1983, the year of his death. But undoubtedly one of the great attractions of the MNCARS is *Guernica*, the heartrending vision portrayed by

Picasso in 1937 of the horror, death and destruction of the Guernica bombardment. Other works of Picasso on show include preparatory sketches for Guernica and *Mujer en azul*. Juan Gris, Pablo Gargallo, Braque, Antoni Tàpies, Chillida, the Equipo Crónica, Francis Bacon, Tony Cragg, Shnabel, Bruce Nauman, Dan Flavin and many other artists also have their place in this museum, that in addition organises important temporary exhibitions.

«El gran masturbador» by Salvador Dalí and «Guernica» by Picasso (Archivo Fotográfico Museo Nacional Centro de Arte Reina Sofía, Madrid).

63

Pond in the El Retiro Park, presided over by the statue of Alfonso XII.

EL RETIRO PARK

This is Madrid's most important park, not because of size (12 hectares) but due to its rich history, as it originally formed part of the Palace of Buen Retiro, constructed in the 17th century by Philip IV. For this, the king employed Italian artists, who conceived the park as a succession of spaces in which plants and trees alternated with ponds, statues or small shrines, forming a veritable labyrinth. This Italian Baroque style was altered in the 18th century with the ascendance to the throne of the Bourbons, from which time on the predominant style employed was of French influence, an example of which is «El Parterre».

The gardens were destroyed during the War of Spanish Succession and began to be reconstructed during the reigns of Ferdinand VII and Isabel II. After the Revolution of September 1868, the nature of the park changed radically, as it became the property of the City Council, and it is now an area where a wide range of leisure activities are available, sailing and rowing in the lake on whose banks stands the monument to Alphonse XII, many types of sports, exhibitions at the **Palace of Velazquez** and in the **Crystal Palace** or, simply, as the site of pleasant, relaxing walks.

The Palace of Velázquez was designed to house the Exhibition of Mining in 1883 and that of Glass some years later, in 1887, and as a tropical greenhouse for an exhibition on the Philipines. Another area of special interest is The Rose Garden, which between April and June offers a selection of different varieties of roses. All around the grounds are set numerous statues: that of the Fallen Angel, the work of Francisco

*Palace of Velázquez
and Crystal Palace, in
El Retiro Park.*

Monument to General Martínez Campos.

Bellver from the end of the 19th century, is the best known, because it is apparently dedicated to the devil, although in reality it is an interpretation of the *Paradise Lost* by Milton; other statues are devoted to famous Spaniards, such as that of General Martínez Campos, the work of Benlliure, considered to be one of the best in Madrid.

To the south of the park, and outside its grounds, is the **National Museum of Anthropology** and the **Astronomical Observatory.** The Observatory was constructed at the initiative of Jorge Juan, who suggested to King Charles III the creation of an Astronomy Lecture Hall to complement the monarch's idea of promoting the sciences, though work was not finally commenced until 1790, during the reign of Charles IV. The building, designed by Villanueva, is one of the purest exponents of Neo-Classicism to be found in Madrid.

Rose Garden in El Retiro Park.

Palacio del Congreso de los Diputados.

THE CONGRESO DE LOS DIPUTADOS AND THE CASA DE LOPE DE VEGA

The **Palacio del Congreso de los Diputados**, seat of the Spanish Parliament, was built on the site of the Church of the Espiritu Santo, where the Cortes had met since 1834. A design by Narciso Pascual y Colomer was chosen for its construction, whose design was inspired by the Italian palaces of the 15th century, with the addition of a Corinthian portico with classical pediment. The first stone was laid by Isabel II in 1843 and the building was completed in 1850. The

Detail of one of the lions flanking the entrance to the Palacio del Congreso de los Diputados.

Casa Museo Lope de Vega.

Teatro de la Comedia.

two lions flanking the entrance were cast in 1860 in metal from cannons captured during the war in Africa. and when this palace with little more accommodation than the Salón de Sesiones, was outgrown alongside it another building was constructed for MP's offices. In the neighbouring street of Cervantes is the museum **Casa Museo Lope de Vega**, where the famous dramatist lived from 1610 to 1635, the year of his death. This house is one of the few examples of dwellings from the early 17th century still extant in Madrid. It has been rehabilitated and furnished with period furnishing, including the cheerful garden in the interior patio, where the same plants have been established as were grown by Lope de Vega, a great garden lover.

Lope de Vega, Calderón de la Barca and Tirso de Molina, the three great figures of the Siglo de Oro in Spanish theatre, left an important theatrical legacy. Their works are continually represented in theatres in the capital and throughout Spain, in particular in the **Teatro de la Comedia**, the home of the National Company of Classical Theatre, in the neighbouring Calle del Príncipe. In this same street can also be found the **Teatro Español**, in operation as such since 1583, although the building dates from the 18th century. Another important theatre in this area is the **Teatro Lírico de la Zarzuela**, in Jovellanos behind the Palacio del Congreso de los Diputados, founded in the mid-18th century, only staging zarzuelas (light operas), the most typical artistic style of Madrid.

View over the first stretch of Gran Vía.

GRAN VIA, PLAZA DE ESPAÑA AND CALLE DE LA PRINCESA

Gran Vía, one of the most animated and commercial through-ways in the city, was already famous in 1862 when it was still at the planning stage, thanks to the zarzuela of the same name. At last, in 1910, work commenced on this road, conceived to connect the districts of Argüelles and Salamanca, and for whose building many houses and small streets were demolished. One building saved from the pickaxe was the **Oratorio del Caballero de Gracia** whose main entrance is in the street that gave it its name. It is built in the most pure Neo-Classical style, particularly beautiful inside, and built by Juan de Villanueva between 1786 and 1795.

The first section of Gran Vía runs between the Alcalá and the fountain of San Luis, was inaugurated in 1924: this is the part that has best conserved the homogeneity of its buildings. Among these are the **Edificio Metrópolis** (1905) next to Alcalá, the work of the Fevrier brothers, and crowned by the sculpture of the *Winged Victory* by Federico Collaut Valera: in 1975, when the building changed hands, this sculpture replaced the Phoenix that had been in pride of place till then; the **Edificio Grassy** (1916) at no. 1, by Eladio Laredo; the **Casa Urquijo** (1917) at no. 6, by José Mª Mendoza y Ussía; the block of dwellings belonging to the insurance company **La Estrella** at no. 10, by Pedro Mathet; the **Hotel Roma** (1913) at no. 18, by Eduardo Reynals; and the **Casino Militar** (1916) at no. 13, by Eduardo Sánchez Eznarriaga.

Great Vía, next to Calle Alcalá.

Aerial view of Gran Vía. ▷

In the second section, up to the Plaza de Callao, a boulevard was planned that in the end was never built. Here you can appreciate the functionalism in its architecture. The building that most draws your attention is that planned by Ignacio Cárdenas with the cooperation of the American Weeks, for **Telefónica**. Completed in 1929, it was the first skyscraper in Madrid, and the permit for its height of 81 metres was only granted because it was declared to be of public utility. Other outstanding buildings are the **Casa Matesanz** (1919) at no. 27, the **Hotel Alfonso XIII** (1920-25) at no. 34, both by Antonio Palacios; the **Madrid-París** building (1920) at no 32, by Teodoro Anasagasti, and the **Hotel Atlántico** (1920) at no. 38, by Joaquín Saldaña.

In the last section, between the Plaza del Callao and the Plaza de España, the buildings are much more varied in character, and bear no relation to each other, with their different heights and styles. The modern style of two of these buildings, both in the Plaza del Callao, merits a comment: the **Palacio de la Prensa**, planned by Pedro Muguruza in 1924, and the **Edificio Carrión**, better known as the Capitol, started in 1931 to a design by Luis Martínez Feduchi and Vicente Eced.

The **Plaza de España** is a huge esplanade whose main functions are as a meeting point, and as a roundabout for traffic. Presiding over its central gardens is the **Monument to Cervantes**, designed in 1915 by Teodoro Anasagasti and Mateo Inurria. Other characteristic features of the square are the two skyscrapers erected in the 1950s to crown Gran Vía, both by the Otamendi brothers: the **Torre de Madrid** and the **Edificio España**. In contrast, in the southern corner of the square, there are two elegant early-20th century palace buildings: the headquarters of the **Real Compañía Asturiana de Minas**, by Manuel Martínez

71

Plaza del Callao.

Plaza de España. ▷

Detail of the monument to Cervantes, in the Plaza de España.

Calle de la Princesa.

74

Main façade of the Palacio de Liria.

Former Barracks of the Conde Duque.

Victory Arch and the buildings of the Airforce Headquarters.

View of the Victory Arch and the Faro de la Moncloa by night. ▷

Angel, and the **Casa Gallardo**, by Federico Arias Rey. The **Calle de la Princesa** was planned as a continuation of Gran Vía under the project for creating an east-west axis perpendicular to la Castellana, and linking up with the Ciudad Universitaria. A very commercial street, of note being the **Palacio de Liria**, considered to be the most beautiful Madrid example of a gentleman's residence. Its construction was commissioned in 1773 by Jacobo Stuart Fitz-James, third Duke of Berwick and Liria, married to the sister of the Duke of Alba, to a design of Sabatini and Ventura Rodríguez. The palace, owned by the House of Alba, brings together an important collection of works of art which can only be seen by prior arrangement.

Just behind the palace is the **Cuartel General del Conde Duque**, a former barracks building of enormous proportions built between 1720 and 1754 by Pedro de Ribera to accommodate the Royal Company of Guards. It is structured around three patios, the central one being the largest, and is made in brick with great decorative simplicity, with the exception of the main façade in carved stone, in which flags, shields and military trophies are portrayed. At present it houses the City Library and several exhibition rooms. At the end of Calle de la Princesa is the **Air Force Headquarters**, started in 1939 by Luis Gutiérrez Soto who took his inspiration from the Baroque style that had traditionally been used in Madrid, and the **Victory Arch**, beyond which is the so-called **Faro de la Moncloa** (Moncloa lighthouse), a new tower that lets you obtain «aerial» type views over Madrid The Victory Arch leads into the area of the Moncloa, the site of the **Palace of the Moncloa**, official residence of the President of the Government, and to the **Ciudad Universitaria**.

Paseo de Recoletos.

Paseo de la Castellana. ▷

PASEO DE RECOLETOS AND PASEO DE LA CASTELLANA

The Paseo de Recoletos and the first section of the Castellana came into being in the 19th century as a result of the northwards expansion of the city. Originating as Passages with an aristocratic and quiet character, this was the preferred setting for the upper-middle classes to build their palaces, today mostly gone or having changed their functions from residences to the housing of financial or official bodies. However, and in spite of the fast traffic circulating on its road, it is still pleasant to stroll through its central gardens or take a soft drink on one of its terraces, particularly lively on summer nights.

A excellent example of the fabulous mansions that in days gone by lined the Paseo de Recoletos is the **Palace of the Marquis of Salamanca**, today headquarters of the Banco Hipotecario, built in Neo Renaissance Italian style in the 1850s. It belonged to a famous character of the Madrid of that time, the Marquis of Salamanca (1811-1883), banker, lawyer, politician and art patron, who led a lively life, amassing large fortunes but also –and this is how he ended his days– passing through great economic hardship. He was the main force behind the district to which he gave his name, that extends to the east of the Paseo de Recoletos, built up from 1860 on, where the richest families in the city set up home. The streets of Velázquez, Príncipe de Vergara and above all Serrano, all very commercial, with elegant designer shops, are the main arteries of the district.

Above the palace, at number 20 of the Paseo de Recoletos, there is an enormous building in the Classicist

Palace of the Marquis of Salamanca.

National Library.

National Archaeological Museum: votive crowns of Guarrazar, the Dama de Elche, the Dama de Baza and Livia de Paestum. (Archivo Fotográfico Museo Arqueológico Nacional).

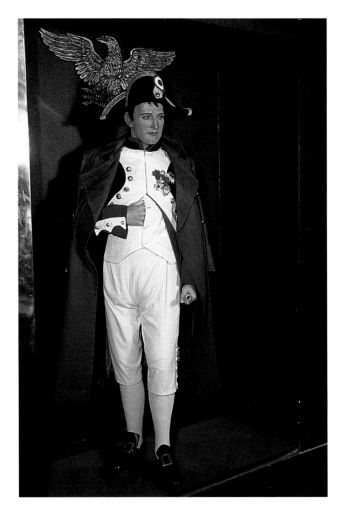

Wax Museum: Napoleon Bonaparte and Saint Teresa of Calcutta with Lady Diana Spencer (Archivo Fotográfico Museo de Cera).

style, started in 1866 by Francisco Jareño and finished in 1892 by Ruiz de Salces, shared by the **National Library** and the **National Archaeological Museum**, this last with its entrance from Calle de Serrano. The National Library was built to replace the Royal Library created by Philip V in 1712. Its collections include more than five million books, manuscripts, incunabulae, leaflets, illustrations, engravings and magazines, the most interesting among which are the codex of *Mío Cid* and the collection of *El Quijote*, with more than 3,000 copies of editions translated into more than 30 languages. The National Archaeological Museum was founded by Isabel II in 1867 with collections coming from different institutions throughout the country. Gradually being extended, its more than 40 rooms offer an authentic chronicle of the Peninsula, from prehis-

tory to the Late Middle Ages. As well as housing an excellent reproduction of the cave paintings of Altamira, it conserves treasures like the three «damas» of Iberian sculpture –La Dama de Elche, La Dama de Baza and La Dama del Cerro de los Santos–, all the votive crowns of Guarrazar, wooden ceilings in Mudejar style carved by Muslim craftsmen, an important numismatic collection, popular ceramics, sarcophagi and Greek and Roman mausoleums, and Greek and Etruscan glasses, among its many other valuable exhibits.

Facing the National Library is the **Wax Museum**, with more than 450 figures of historical and famous people, in addition to a scary «horror train», and immediately afterwards we come to the **Plaza de Colón**.

Aerial view of the Plaza de Colón.

83

Monument to Colón and Torres de Colón.

The Gardens of the Discovery occupy the centre of the square, presided over, on the east side, by huge allegorical sculptures by Vaquero Turcios, representing the heroic voyage of Columbus. In one corner of the square is the Neo-Gothic monument to that explorer, designed by Arturo Melida in 1885. Below the square is the **Centro Cultural de la Villa de Madrid**, hidden behind a beautiful and noisy curtain of water. The centre contains a concert hall, exhibition rooms and a theatre for social and cultural events. Lastly, since 1976 one side of the square has housed the so-called **Torres de Colón**, two high buildings, both the work of architect Antonio Lamela.

Starting at the Plaza de Colón, the Paseo de Recoletos changes its name to Paseo de la Castellana. Shortly before arriving at the **Glorieta de Emilio Castelar**, dedicated to this politician and writer (1832-1899), and next to Calle de Juan Bravo, is the **Outdoor Sculpture Museum**, a garden where many sculptures by Spanish avant-garde artists are exhibited: Julio González, Manuel Rivera, Andrés Alfaro, Eusebio Sempere, Eduardo Chillida and Joan Miró, among others. Further north on the Castellana there are other interesting museums, the **National Museum of the Natural Sciences**, with replicas of dinosaurs, giant skeletons and extensive anthropological and mineral collections. It is housed in a building in Neo Mudejar style built in 1881 by Fernando de la Torriente as a Palace for Industry and the Arts. Opposite the museum are some pleasant gardens adorned with the **Monument to Isabel la Católica and to the Constitution**, and behind the museum, the famous **Residencia de Estudiantes** (student residence), which gave lodgings to Federico García Lorca, Luis Buñuel, Salvador Dalí and Juan Ramón Jiménez, among others.

National Museum of the Natural Sciences.

Monument to Isabel la Católica.

85

Two views of the Plaza de San Juan de la Cruz.

The Azca Complex, an example Madrid's avant-garde architecture.

Further on, next to the Plaza de San Juan de la Cruz and on the former site of the Madrid Hippodrome, various buildings were erected in the 1930s in a very functional style of architecture. They were meant to house government offices known as the **Nuevos Ministerios**, but were not completed until after the Civil War, and were then inaugurated in 1958 as the Ministry of Public Works. From here on, a new section of the Castellana begins, that has seen new constructions during recent years. The most notable of these are some buildings and skyscrapers on spectacular lines such as the **Azca Complex**, a large block containing the **Torre Picasso**, 150 m and 43 storeys high, designed by Minoru Yamasaki; the **Torre de Europa**, of circular shape and with 31 storeys; and the **BBVA building**, work of Sáinz de Oíza; and at its most northerly point, next to the Plaza de Castilla, the Puerta de Europa, better known as **Torres Puerta de**

Europa, two large glass blocks inclined towards the interior of the passage. Tucked in among these are two other important buildings, the **Palace of Exhibitions and Conferences**, built in 1964 and whose façade has been decorated since 1980 with a mural by Joan Miró; and the **Santiago Bernabeu Football Stadium**, headquarters of Real Madrid CF, inaugurated in 1947. The other great football stadium in Madrid, the Vicente Calderón, headquarters of Atlético de Madrid, is to be found beside the Manzanares River, not far from the Puerta de Toledo.

The final section of the Castellana, from the Plaza de Castilla, will be changing its appearance shortly under an ambitious plan that will equip this area with parks, squares and even more spectacular buildings. This plan will also affect **Chamartín Station**, Madrid's busiest railway station, which will be extended to practically double its current surface area.

Torre Picasso.

Azca Complex, Torre de
Europa. ▷

Torres Puerta de Europa.

Palace of Exhibitions and Conferences.

*Santiago Bernabeu
football stadium.*

*Vicente Calderón
football stadium.*

Manzanares River.

THE MANZANARES AND ITS BRIDGES

Several bridges cross the Manzanares, among which two are of special interest.

The most imposing, and the bridge that in its day was the butt of literary jokes due to its monumental qualities, in the face of the small dimensions of the river, then as now, is the **Puente de Segovia**. Its building was ordered by Philip II who, after establishing his capital in Spain, wanted to give it suitably grand buildings. It was opened in 1584 and designed by Juan de Herrera. It follows austere lines, with no more decoration than the Renaissance rhythm of its arches and the typical Horseshoe Balls

on its parapets. The **Puente de Toledo**, the other historical bridge of Madrid, was constructed during the reign of Philip V, though its true sponsor was the Marquis of Vadillo, mayor of the city from 1715 to 1729, who realised the need to replace the old wooden bridge crossing the river at this busy point to facilitate the entrance of supplies to the city from La Mancha. Pedro de Ribera was commissioned with the construction of the bridge in his characteristic Baroque style. The granite monument is formed by five equal arches with, on either side of the central arch, two fine niches containing statues of San Isidro and Santa María de la Cabeza, by Juan Ron.

Puente de Segovia.

Puente de Toledo.

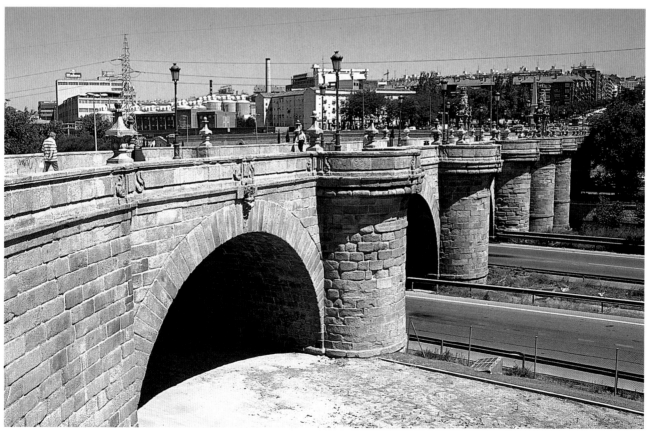

Hermitage of San Isidro.

THE HERMITAGES OF MADRID AND OTHER CHURCHES OF INTEREST

The most famous is the **Hermitage of San Isidro**, not so much for its artistic quality as for the popular procession that takes place there on the day of its saint, the 15th of May, a procession whose atmosphere is portrayed in numerous works of Goya. It is set on what used to be the land worked by San Isidro and where, according to tradition, the saint made a spring of miraculous water burst out of the ground.

The **Hermitage of the Virgen del Puerto**, situated between the river and the Gardens of the Campo de Moro, was built in 1718, commissioned by the Marquis of Vadillo, co-alderman of the City, from Pedro de Ribera, to let the laundry workers who worked on the banks of the Manzanares attend mass.

The **Hermitage of San Antonio de la Florida**, situated next to the river and the Parque del Oeste, was built during the reign of Charles IV by Philip Fontanam in Neo-Classical style. This is the most interesting of all due to the frescos that decorate its interior, executed in 1798 by Francisco de Goya, and one of his most captivating works. So as to preserve them in the best possible condition, in 1928 a twin hermitage was built beside it for daily use, with the original building being converted into a museum.

Other interesting churches not mentioned in earlier chapters are the **Church of the Salesas Reales**, the only remains of a vast convent commissioned in the mid-18th century by Bárbara de Braganza, wife of Ferdinand VI, to house a college for daughters of nobility. It now holds the tombs of these monarchs, in accordance with their disapproval of the custom of burying members of the royal family in the monastery of El Escorial; and the **Church of San Antonio de los Alemanes**, from the 17th century, with beautiful fresco decorations by Luca Giordano on its great vault, and by Francisco de Ricci and Juan Carreño on its dome.

Hermitage of the Virgen del Puerto.

Hermitage of San Antonio de la Florida, with frescos on dome and vaults by Francisco de Goya.

Church of the Salesas Reales. ▷

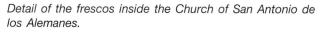

Detail of the frescos inside the Church of San Antonio de los Alemanes.

Parque del Oeste.

PARKS OF MADRID

The centre of Madrid has a great number of parks, containing many different types of landscapes: romantic, rural, open grasslands, woods and flower-beds. In addition to the parks of El Retiro, the Campos del Moro, Sabatini and the Botanical Gardens already described, three more must be mentioned: the Parque del Oeste, the Casa de Campo and El Capricho.

In the **Parque del Oeste** there are three very different areas, one large profusely planted area, the area of the Rose Garden, and the so-called gardens of the mountain of Prince Pío whose name makes reference to the holiday palace that Prince Pío of

Savoy had here. It was on this hill that the executions by firing squad took place on the 3rd of May 1808 that are recalled for posterity in the famous canvas by Goya. Since 1970 this mountains has been presided over by the **Templo de Debod**, built by the Pharaoh Azekheramon in the 4th century B.C. in honour of the god Amon, and donated by the Egyptian government to Spain in gratitude for their cooperation in the work of rescuing the monuments of the valley of Nubia affected by the construction of the Aswan Dam. In the Rose Garden area, a cable railway takes you to the centre of Casa de Campo.

With its almost 1,800 hectares, the **Casa de Campo** is the largest park in Madrid. Its origins date back to the reign of Philip II, who acquired these lands

*Parque del Oeste.
sculpture in the area of
The Rose Garden.*

Templo de Debod.

Gardens of the Casa de Campo: lake and Amusement Park.

for the royal hunt. In 1931, by a decision of the Second Republic, it came into city ownership. Today it includes areas with differing facilities, such as the **Geological Park**, the **Entertainments Park** and the **Trade Fair Buildings**, as well as numerous picnic areas round its lake, in which boats are available.

El Capricho is a bustling park situated to the east of the city, near the Avenida de América. It was laid out towards the end of the 18th century by the Duchess of Osuna. It has a large lake with an octagonal-shaped pavilion for dancing, as well as many statues and fountains and other interesting features, including a bandstand dedicated to Baco and a summerhouse given over to the breeding of bees. The former holiday house of the Duchess of Osuna is also preserved, although its façade was totally remodelled in 1835 by Martín López Aguado.

Parque de El Capricho.

«Noria, Jávea» and «Autorretrato» by Sorolla (Archivo Fotográfico Museo Sorolla).

MUSEUMS OF MADRID

The list of museums in Madrid is extremely long; some of these like El Prado would on their own justify a visit to the capital. Other art museums have already been mentioned throughout this book, but there are still more to be noted. These include the **Museo Sorolla** (Paseo General Martínez Campos 37, in the house where the painter had his studio, and containing most of his work and that of his painter friends), the **Museo Cerralbo** (Ventura Rodríguez 17, with more than 50,000 pieces from all fields from the private collection made by the Marquis of Cerralbo throughout his life, and exhibited in the delightful rooms of a palace built for the purpose at the end of the 19th century); the **Museo de la Fundación Lázaro Galdiano** (Serrano 122, also boasts a valuable collection of diverse pieces that were collected by this publisher and writer, and which are housed in what was his residence, a beautiful early

Museo Cerralbo:
Stairway of Honour and
Music Room
(Photos: Museo Cerralbo).

Museum of the
Fundación Lázaro
Galdiano.

20th century villa), the **Museo Romántico** (San Mateo 13, set up in a building that dates from the end of the 18th century, whose rooms evoke the artistic, literary and folkloric environment of the Romantic era, an important art gallery for this period and with curious pieces such as the gun with which the famous satirist Mariano José de Larra committed suicide); and the **Museo de América** (Avenida Reyes Católicos 6, with one of the most comprehensive collections in the world of pre-Columbian art, including such extraordinary pieces as the Treasure of the Quimbaya, from Colombia, or the Tro-Cortesiano Codex, the largest Maya codex still extant).

Those interested in the history of the city have in the **Museum of the City** (Prince of Vergara 32) and the **Municipal Museum** (Fuencarral 78), an extensive collection of painting, engravings, plans and photographs of Madrid throughout the ages. This last museum to be mentioned also has the added attraction of being housed in an exceptional building, considered the master work of Pedro de Ribera, built between 1722 and 1799 as a Hospice. Its most striking feature is its spectacular main façade, characterised by the exuberance of the decorative elements which are typical of this architect. An image of San Fernando presides over this riot of decoration.

Finally, reference must be made to two museums covering the technical field, the Museum of the Air and the Railway Museum, not forgetting the **Madrid Planetarium**, situated in the Park de Tierno Galván. Inaugurated in 1981 and extended on various occasions in recent years, the **Museum of the Air** (carretera de Extremadura km 10.6) shows in its 60,000 m² of exhibition 156 airships of all eras, and a host of objects and documents giving the history of Spanish aviation, as well as the evolution and progress of aero-space techniques, collections that have made it into one of the five most important of its kind in the world. The **National Railway Museum** (Paseo de las Delicias 61) in the former station of Las Delicias, closed to railway traffic since 1971, exhibits an extensive inventory of trains, models, engravings and other objects such as the most diverse equipment used in trains and stations, that tells us the history of the railway in Spain since its origins to the present day.

City Museum.

Madrid Planetarium.

*Museum of the Air:
Dornier hydroplane
DO-24 HD-5.*

Couples dancing the schottische in the Plaza Mayor.

POPULAR FESTIVITIES AND BULLFIGHTS

The inhabitants of Madrid have always been great lovers of street festivities to celebrate important dates. On 5 January is the Procession of the Magi, which follows a route through all the main streets of the city, and in February, Carnival officially commences with the inaugural address of the Muse of this fiesta, who also presides over the procession along La Castellana and Recoletos, with prizes for the best floats. During this festivity, there are joke telling competitions and dances organised by the City Council, and Carnival ends on Ash Wednesday with the Burial of the Sardine, which is accompanied by a mournful procession.

At Easter, many processions take place, outstanding of which are: those of the Poor Jesus, the Great Power and the Macarena on the Thursday; those of Jesus of Medinaceli, the Dolorosa and the Silence on Good Friday, when the Christ Procession also takes place in the cloisters of the Convent of the Descalzas, led by a magnificent wooden statue by Gaspar Becerra; and, lastly, on Easter Saturday, the Holy Burial, which takes place in Plaza Mayor.

On 2 May is the commemoration of the Autonomous Community of Madrid, with the organisation of numerous cultural and leisure activities, but the most important festivities take place on May 15, day of San Isidro, patron saint of the city, with concerts, theatre perfor-

mances, puppet shows and passacaglias, book and craft fairs, dances lasting well into the early hours and firework displays. All this in stark contrast with the day of the other patron saint of the city, that of the Virgin of the Almudena (November 9), which passes by practically unnoticed.

At the beginning of December, the city begins to prepare for the Christmas festivities, after which the population sees the old year out on 31 December to the chimes of the clock in the Puerta del Sol. The New Year is welcomed with particular enthusiasm by the crowd gathered in this square.

Throughout the year, fiestas are celebrated in the various barrios or districts of Madrid, of which the most outstanding and traditional are: that of Saint Anthony of La Florida, on 13 June; those of the Virgin of Carmen, on 16 July; and those of Saint Cayetano, Saint Lawrence and La Paloma in the first half of August.

Since medieval times, the most popular entertainment in Madrid has been bullfighting. In the 17th century, every opportunity was taken to hold bullfights in the Plaza Mayor and in 1754 King Ferdinand VI commissioned the architects Ventura Rodríguez and Francisco Moradillo to build a bullring to hold twelve thousand spectators. By the early-20th century, this ring was found to be too small to hold all those wishing to attend the national fiesta and the bullring of the **Plaza Monumental de las Ventas** was constructed by José Espelius and Manuel Muñoz Monasterio, who designed it in the Mudejar style characteristic of many bullrings, with brick walls and ceramic decoration. With a capacity of 22,000, it is the largest in Spain and is also considered the most important, the top bullfighters appearing here as if taking an exam before a demanding and knowledgeable crowd. Between 70 and 72 bullfights are held at «Las Ventas» every year, the season beginning in April, but the high point is during the San Isidro Fair, when the ring holds capacity audiences for a total of 26 bullfights, three of which are usually with young bulls and another two on horseback. After the Fair, bullfights continue to be held every Sunday and on some important holidays, the most important events being the Charity and Press corridas. The season ends with the four or five bullfights of the Autumn Fair.

Procession of the Eucharist.

Plaza Monumental de las Ventas.

The Biscuit Seller, typical figure of Madrid.

GASTRONOMY

There are a number of fine dishes which, although they originated in other areas, have become typical of Madrid and can now be considered local. *Cocido*, stew, is the most typical dish of the city, followed by *gallinejas*, fried pieces of chicken, *entresijos*, similar to tripe, snails, garlic soups (unlike in other parts of Spain, cooked without egg) and, turning to sweets, *churros* and *porras*, dough deep-fried in batter, and San Isidro doughnuts. The finest local drinks include wines from San Martin de Valdeiglesias, Colmenar de Oreja and Arganda and the distinctive liquor made from madrona.

Besides the typical dishes, Madrid also offers specialities from all the regions of Spain and from other countries, and although it seems paradoxical, it has one of the main fish markets in the world and, in many people's opinion, it is the best place in the country to eat fish. Depending on one's pocket, it is possible to choose between a five-star restaurant and the cheapest businessman's lunch. Or, more informally, to eat «tapas» at any of the infinity of taverns, beer-houses and bars to be found all over the city.

Typical dishes, examples of Madrid cuisine: stew, tripe and chocolate with churros.

Royal Palace of El Pardo (Copyright © Patrimonio Nacional).

SURROUNDINGS OF MADRID

Around Madrid you will find the majority of the so-called Royal Sites, palaces and monuments, now in State ownership but meant for the use and service of the King and the members of the Royal Family. This is the case with the Royal Palace in Madrid, which can be visited with the exception of the days when official events are being held.

The nearest to Madrid, only some 14 km to the north, is the **Royal Palace of El Pardo**, set on the El Pardo Mountain, a former royal hunting ground with more than 16,000 hectares of woods, and since the Middle Ages the setting of the holiday homes of the monarch. Henry IV ordered the building of a small castle that Charles V rebuilt in 1553, but which burnt down in 1604 making a new construction necessary. The palace was later extended by successive monarchs. Ferdinand VI closed off the whole perimeter of the Mountain, building the Puerta de Hierro and the bridge of San Fernando as an entrance to the Royal Site. In 1772 Charles III commissioned Sabatini to make a new extension, giving it its present-day appearance, and also at the same time decorating its rooms with the paintings, tapestries, furniture, lights and clocks preserved here today. Outstanding are the tapestries on board by Goya, who carried out five of his best known series for this palace, and pictures like the portrait of Isabel la Católica, Juan of Flanders, and of Don Juan José of Austria on horseback, by Ribera. After the Civil War, El Pardo was the residence of General Franco until his death, being reformed after 1983 as a museum and residence of foreign Heads of State on official visits.

In the area of the El Pardo Mountain, other buildings were constructed, such as the **Palace of the Zarzuela**, official residence of Their Majesties the King and Queen, which can not be visited; the **Casita del Principe**, **the Quinta del Duque de Arco**, with its delightful gardens, and the **Convent of the Capuchins**. The latter, founded by Philip III, holds a Reclining Christ carved by Gregorio Fernández, considered to be one of the

Puerta de Hierro.

master works of this 17th century Spanish maker of religious images.

49 km to the south of Madrid is the **Royal Palace of Aranjuez**. Its construction was begun by Philip II with the same architects as El Escorial, Juan Bautista de Toledo and Juan de Herrera, Completed in the times of Ferdinand VI it was further extended with two wings by Charles III, who commissioned Sabatini for these works. It boasts public rooms that are richly adorned with furniture, tapestries and paintings largely from the 18th century, outstanding among which is the Gabinete de Porcelana, with walls and ceiling lined with sheets of porcelain made in the Royal Factories of the Buen Retiro. Just as interesting, or even more so, is a visit to the marvellous gardens at the Casa de Marineros, with its **Museum of Royal Feluccas** (sailing boats), and the Casita del Labrador, a most beautiful Neo-Classical building by Juan de Villanueva.

Portrait of Isabel la Católica by Juan de Flandes, in the Royal Palace of El Pardo (Copyright © Patrimonio Nacional).

Royal Palace of
Aranjuez *(Copyright
© Patrimonio Nacional).*

Royal Palace of
Aranjuez: Statue gallery
of the Casita del
Labrador *(Copyright ©
Patrimonio Nacional).*

Royal Monastery of San Lorenzo in El Escorial (Copyright © Patrimonio Nacional).

Royal Monastery of San Lorenzo in El Escorial: Sala de las Batallas (Copyright © Patrimonio Nacional).

The **Royal Monastery of San Lorenzo in El Escorial**, 49 km west of Madrid, at the foot of the Guadarrama Mountains, declared Heritage of Humanity in 1984, was the political centre of the empire of Philip II. It was here that he organised his palace and famous library, and it is also his mausoleum and that of his parents, relatives and successors to the throne, as well as housing the great basilica and monastery. Its building was carried out between 1562 and 1584 to designs of Juan Bautista de Toledo and Juan de Herrera, and the rooms of the palace and also the monastery were decorated by Italian painters summoned by Philip II, among whom Zuccaro, Tibaldi and Cambiaso merit special mention. Similarly, within its walls it holds works by great artists such as Bosch, El Greco, Claudio Coello, Velázquez and Monegro. In what is known as the Palace of the Bourbons there is an important set of tapestries on board by Goya.

Of special interest in its gardens are the Casita del Príncipe or that of Abajo (Below), and the Casita del Infante or that of Arriba (Above), from which you can admire a beautiful panorama of the monastery, both built between 1771 and 1773 by Juan de Villanueva. Not far from El Escorial, in the valley of Cuelgamuros, and in the years following the Civil War, General Franco ordered the building of the monument known as the **Valley of the Fallen**, whose most spectacular feature is the immense cross, 150 metres high, that crowns the monument. Carved into the rock is the great sepulchral basilica, where the General and various fallen of the two opposing sides in the civil war are buried.

Lastly, mention must be made of the towns of **Alcalá de Henares**, whose famous University and historical centre were declared Heritage of Humanity in 1998, and **Chinchón**, with its preserved 19th century palace and original Plaza Mayor.

Valley of the Fallen (Copyright © Patrimonio Nacional).

Façade of the University of Alcalá de Henares.

Plaza Mayor of Chinchón.

115

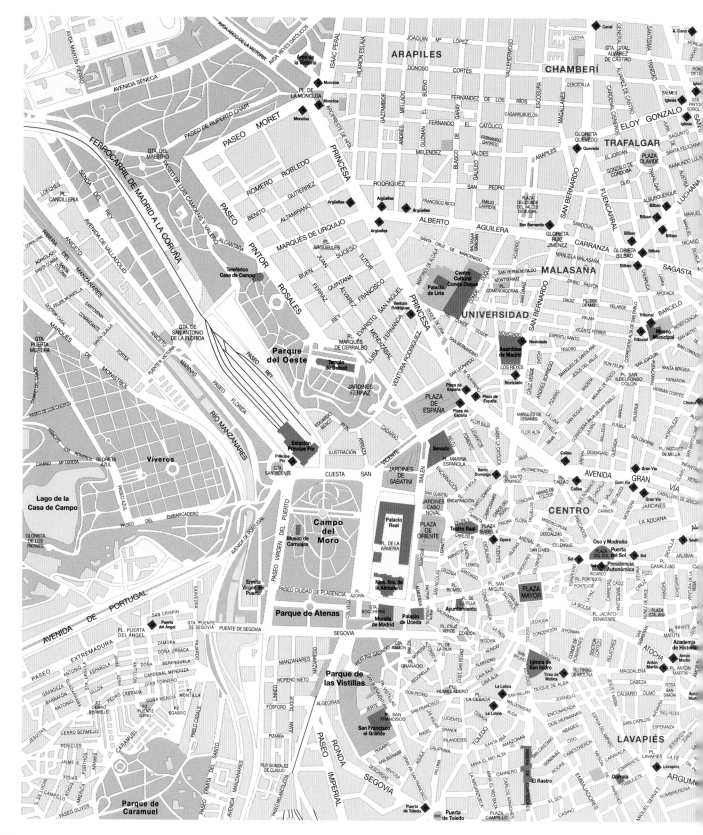

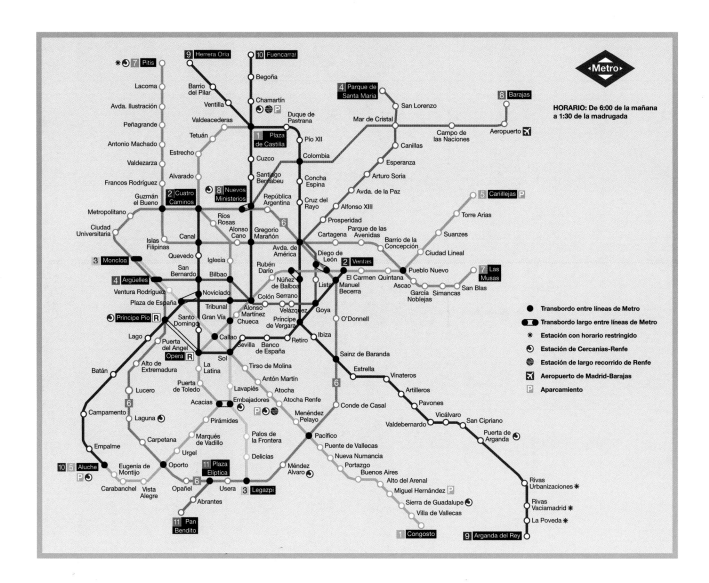

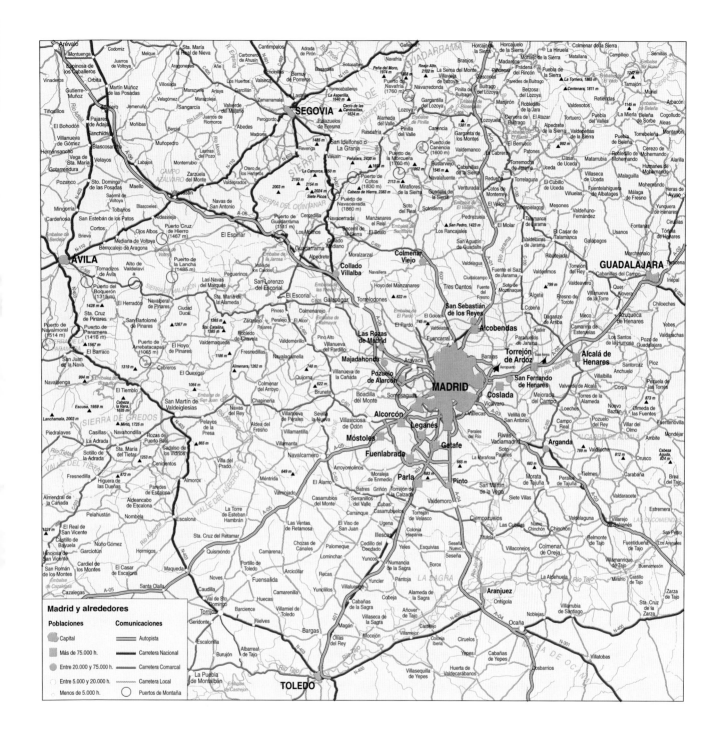

Madrid y alrededores

Poblaciones

- Capital
- Más de 75.000 h.
- Entre 20.000 y 75.000 h.
- Entre 5.000 y 20.000 h.
- Menos de 5.000 h.

Comunicaciones

- Autopista
- Carretera Nacional
- Carretera Comarcal
- Carretera Local
- Puertos de Montaña

CONTENTS

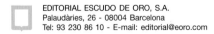

EDITORIAL ESCUDO DE ORO, S.A.
Palaudàries, 26 - 08004 Barcelona
Tel: 93 230 86 10 - E-mail: editorial@eoro.com

I.S.B.N. 84-378-2373-0
Printed by FISA - Escudo de Oro, S.A.
Legal Dep. B. 12251-2002

Protegemos el bosque; papel procedente de cultivos forestales controlados
Wir schützen den Wald. Papier aus kontrollierten Forsten.
We protect our forests. The paper used comes from controlled forestry plantations
Nous sauvegardons la forêt: papier provenant de cultures forestières contrôlées